THIS IS ME! ACROSTICS

Words Of Imagination

Edited By Roseanna Caswell

First published in Great Britain in 2024 by:

Young Writers
Remus House
Coltsfoot Drive
Peterborough
PE2 9BF
Telephone: 01733 890066
Website: www.youngwriters.co.uk

All Rights Reserved
Book Design by Ashley Janson
© Copyright Contributors 2024
Softback ISBN 978-1-83565-337-1

Printed and bound in the UK by BookPrintingUK
Website: www.bookprintinguk.com
YB0MA0046C

Foreword

Welcome Reader,

For Young Writers' latest competition *This Is Me Acrostics*, we asked primary school pupils to look inside themselves, to think about what makes them unique, and then write an acrostic poem about it! They rose to the challenge magnificently and the result is this fantastic collection of poems, celebrating them and the things that are important to them.

Here at Young Writers our aim is to encourage creativity in children and to inspire a love of the written word, so it's great to get such an amazing response, with some absolutely fantastic poems. It's important for children to focus on and celebrate themselves and this competition allowed them to write freely and honestly, celebrating what makes them great, expressing their hopes and fears, or simply writing about their favourite things. *This Is Me Acrostics* gave them the power of words.

I'd like to congratulate all the young poets in this anthology, I hope this inspires them to continue with their creative writing.

Contents

Albert Pritchard Infant School, Wednesbury

Kai Rafiq (6)   1

Banff Primary School, Banff

Elijus Kaminskis (7)	2
Myah Connell (7)	3
Max Thomson (7)	4
Casey Simpson (7)	5

Beancross Primary School, Grangemouth

Kai Thomson (7)	6
Regan Doherty (7)	7
Noah Jeffrey (7)	8

Cookridge Primary School, Leeds

Matty (7)	9
Evelyn Duffin (6)	10
Lydia Sellars (5)	11

Craigclowan Preparatory School, Perth

Xander Lyburn (7)   12

Craigentinny Primary School, Edinburgh

Aroush Aslam (7)	13
Saara Saini (7)	14
Isabella Sargenti-Joergensen (6)	15
Colt Smith (7)	16

Jordan Baillie (7)	17
Kuba Perzak (7)	18
Zien Almehbash (7)	19
Khaled Khawli (7)	20

Errington Primary School, Redcar

Alfie Kasper (6)	21
Ted Craddy (6)	22

Forster Park Primary School, Catford

Bezalel Olatunde (7)	23
Innaya Hadbur (6)	24
Jaali Rumble (7)	25
Cezar Cazacu (6)	26
Jaden Ogbuehi (6)	27
Denis Kaja (6)	28
Tiwalola Abolarin (6)	29

Grayshott CE Primary School, Grayshott

Yasmin Appleton (6)   30

Hareleeshill Primary School, Larkhall

Jamie Pinchbeck (7)   31

Hermitage Primary School, Hermitage

Layla Colby (7)	32
Ana Laura Hawkins (6)	33

Latchford St James CE Primary School, Warrington

Georgia Clarke (6)	34
Mia Ko (7)	35

Londonderry Primary School, Newtownards

Isabella Gabbey (6)	36
Max Johnson (6)	37
Niko Newell (6)	38

Low Port Primary School, Linlithgow

Maisie Bryce (7)	39
Blaine Brodie (7)	40
Maili MacKenzie (7)	41
Isla Park (6)	42
Eva Ogg (7)	43
Max Meecham (7)	44
Zac Buchanan (7)	45

Millbank Primary School, Buckie

Lillianna Holmes (7)	46
Maddison Smith (7)	47
Logan Mitchell (6)	48
Bria Hildreth (7)	49

Moldgreen Community Primary, Moldgreen

Julian Bueno Sanchez (6)	50
Maksymilian Pisarczyk (6)	51
Sophie Elliott (6)	52
Dayan Ravesh (6)	53
Miracle Ayeni (6)	54
Inayah Akhtar (7)	55
Kenzie Atkinson (6)	56
Lily Rose Mitchell (6)	57
Cole Dyer (6)	58
Mahnoor Fatima (6)	59

North Crescent Primary School, Wickford

Açelya Ecem Aziz (7)	60
Zachary DeLeon (6)	61

Oak View Primary & Nursery School, Hatfield

Jake Crowe (6)	62

Park Lane Primary School, Tilehurst

Archie Sarvar (6)	63
Darcie Hook (6)	64

Parkhill Primary School, Leven

Edwin Libin (5)	65

Parkinson Lane Community Primary School, Halifax

Amelia Butt (5)	66
Aminah Ali (6)	67
Sana Elcarazeh (7)	68
Shan Abdulla (6)	69
Armaan Moghul (5)	70
Inayah Hussain (5)	71
Hoorain Hassan (5)	72

Robsack Wood Primary Academy, St Leonards-On-Sea

Lilliana Money (6)	73
Alfie Goldsmith (6)	74

Seaton School, Aberdeen

Hawwa Alshareef (7)	75
David Emmanuel (7)	76
Tymofii Karpenko (7)	77
Leo Wilson (6)	78

St George's Primary School, Glasgow

Ayyan Malik (6)	79
Ella Mae McNicol (6)	80
Eva Minalescu (7)	81
Harry Carey (7)	82
Ethan (6)	83

St Joseph's Primary School, Gabalfa

Leona Baos (7)	84
Divine Esuku (7)	85
Zoe Ekere (6)	86

St Michael With St Thomas Primary School, Widnes

Evie Fox (6)	87
Lexi Davies (7)	88

St Patrick's Primary School, Eskra

Michaela McGirr (6)	89
Cadhan Gallagher (6)	90

St Philip's CE Primary School, Atherton

Olivia Fox (6)	91
Isaac Calderbank (7)	92

St Stephen's CE Primary School, West Bowling

Ali Saddique (7)	93
Mohammad Hanzalah (6)	94
Ehab Sanattin (6)	95
Haris Akhtar (6)	96
Sara Al-Hourani (7)	97

Struthers Primary School, Muirhead

Corry Gray (7)	98
Lewis Ritchie	99
Lochlan Keenan (7)	100
Callum Wilson (8)	101
Phoebe Coxon (7)	102
Max Wilson (8)	103
Zara Townsend	104

The John Wallis CE Academy, Kingsnorth

Laila Jasim (5)	105
Dane Court (5)	106
Adam Miah (5)	107

Windale Primary School, Greater Leys

Amerleigh Feeley (7)	108
Cordell Massey-Matthews (6)	109
Leonardo Hyseni-Curtis (6)	110
Ali Nasir (6)	111

The Acrostics

Happy

H appy me
A wesome at earning certificates
P ie is not apple pie
P ie is not apple pie, it's Kai pie
Y ay! I'm flying!

Kai Rafiq (6)
Albert Pritchard Infant School, Wednesbury

Horses

H orses are so cute
O nly eat grass
R iding on a horse
S itting on horses
E very horse is my favourite
S ome like to play in the mud.

Elijus Kaminskis (7)
Banff Primary School, Banff

Happy

H aving fun
A nd being with my friends
P laying in the park
P ushing on the swings
Y ou should always feel happy.

Myah Connell (7)
Banff Primary School, Banff

Play

P lay with my friends
L ook at me
A party when I went home
Y ay! I'm playing with Lego.

Max Thomson (7)
Banff Primary School, Banff

Bingo

B ingo is a game
I s fun
N umbers go high
G ive a shout
O ne bingo win.

Casey Simpson (7)
Banff Primary School, Banff

This Is Me

T he bad weather makes me sad because I can't get outside
H ot coffee is the best at waking me up!
I 'm a boy and I love cake, especially chocolate cake
S nakes are my second favourite animal 'cause they are so slippery

I like Peppa Pig because it makes me laugh
S unny days make me want to play football

M y family is the best because we love each other
E very day in school I like my class because we do fun things.

Kai Thomson (7)
Beancross Primary School, Grangemouth

Regan

R ainbows are my favourite thing because they make me happy
E ggs make omelettes and they are my favourite, especially with cheese
G rannies live five minutes away and I see them all the time
'A n apple a day, keeps the doctor away' is my favourite saying
N ature is my favourite and I have to help save the whole world!

Regan Doherty (7)
Beancross Primary School, Grangemouth

Noah

N ovember is my birthday
O range is one of my favourite colours
A ll of my family supports Rangers
H elp other people.

Noah Jeffrey (7)
Beancross Primary School, Grangemouth

All About Me

A pples are my favourite.
L ike playing with my friend.
L ike playing outside.

A t Turkey, I went to a restaurant.
B ye Mum.
O ats are my favourite.
U nder my bed, there are lots of cobwebs.
T rains are fast.

M y sister and I are playing outside.
E very day I play with my toys.

Matty (7)
Cookridge Primary School, Leeds

All About Me

A rtistic and creative.
L ove my friends and family.
L ove science and drawing too.

A mazing at drawing.
B rave.
O utside I play outside.
U nselfish.
T alented at drawing.

M ummy and Daddy are kind.
E xcellent at baking.

Evelyn Duffin (6)
Cookridge Primary School, Leeds

I Am Lydia

A wesome at dancing
L ikes eating chicken drumsticks
L oves mint choc chip.

A mazing at riding her bike
B eautiful
O utstanding
U nique
T alks a lot.

M akes people giggle
E njoys being with her friend.

Lydia Sellars (5)
Cookridge Primary School, Leeds

All About Me

X ander likes football
A lligators are my third favourite animal
N othing stops me
D olphins are my fifth favourite animal
E very day, I like to play football
R unning is my sixth favourite sport.

Xander Lyburn (7)
Craigclowan Preparatory School, Perth

Gymnastics

G ymnastics is cool
Y es, gymnastics is good
M y mum loves gymnastics
N ew moves every day
A pples after gymnastics
S o good at cartwheels
T ricks are fun
I 'm happy to do gymnastics
C ats can't do gymnastics
S o excited to go on a gymnastics holiday.

Aroush Aslam (7)
Craigentinny Primary School, Edinburgh

Swimming

S wimming with me
W ith my friends
I n the pool
M um swims in the pool with me
M um plays in the pool with me
I n the pool, I am having fun
N ow, I am so happy
G oing to the pool with my friend.

Saara Saini (7)
Craigentinny Primary School, Edinburgh

Spidey

S hoots webs
P ounces over cars
I n disguise
D ashes to help people
E verybody loves him
R uns between buildings

M akes the city safe
A lways helpful
N ever bad.

Isabella Sargenti-Joergensen (6)
Craigentinny Primary School, Edinburgh

Star Wars

S tar Wars is cool
T rips to planets
A Stormtrooper is coming
R ed lightsaber

W ar with Kylo Ren
A nakin Skywalker is a Jedi
R eally amazing films
S cary Darth Vader.

Colt Smith (7)
Craigentinny Primary School, Edinburgh

Big Brother

B aby brother on the way
R oman will be his name
O h, I will love him
T iny toes
H elping out
E arly morning cuddles
R eady to be a big brother.

Jordan Baillie (7)
Craigentinny Primary School, Edinburgh

Football

F ast football
O n the grass
O r on the mud
T ackling and running
B ig kicks
A lways training
L ots of fun
L et's score a goal.

Kuba Perzak (7)
Craigentinny Primary School, Edinburgh

Sports

S wimming and practising
P ing-pong
O n the bench doing push-ups
R unning in a race
T ennis is my favourite game
S peed is hard work.

Zien Almehbash (7)
Craigentinny Primary School, Edinburgh

I Love Lego

L ego is fun
E veryone can play
G reat building
O n my bedroom floor.

Khaled Khawli (7)
Craigentinny Primary School, Edinburgh

Alfie

A pples are delicious
L ollipops are my favourite
F unny
I am smart
E xcellent at riding my bike.

Alfie Kasper (6)
Errington Primary School, Redcar

Ted

T eddies are my favourite
E xcellent at football
D on't wake me up!

Ted Craddy (6)
Errington Primary School, Redcar

Brilliant Bezi

B eautiful, tasty, tropical juice
E xcellent, lovely, pretty indigo
Z ippy, super, fast me
A mazing, quiet parents
L ovely, fantastic uncle
E xcellent working guy
L iking my lovely teacher.

Bezalel Olatunde (7)
Forster Park Primary School, Catford

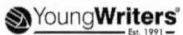

About Me

I mportant family is to me
N oisy class
N ice teacher
A mazing fancy dress
Y ummy pizza
A mazing friend.

Innaya Hadbur (6)
Forster Park Primary School, Catford

Jaali

J uicy apple
A ngry when not playing
A mazing PlayStation
L ovely food
I nteresting friends.

Jaali Rumble (7)
Forster Park Primary School, Catford

This Is Me

C ool,
E xcellent me.
Z ippy adventurer.
A mazing me in the
R ed room, a cool class!

Cezar Cazacu (6)
Forster Park Primary School, Catford

Jaden

J uggling balls
A mazing mom
D angerous things
E xcellent Lego
N oisy elephant.

Jaden Ogbuehi (6)
Forster Park Primary School, Catford

Denis

D angerous lion
E xcellent pizza
N oisy school
I nteresting mum
S unny day.

Denis Kaja (6)
Forster Park Primary School, Catford

Terrific Tiwalola

T errific girl
I nteresting brother
W onderful mother
A mazing father.

Tiwalola Abolarin (6)
Forster Park Primary School, Catford

Yasmin

Y ellow is my happy colour
A nimals cheer me up
S un warms my skin
M ummy and Daddy love me so much
I love them too!
N ow, can I have a hug?

Yasmin Appleton (6)
Grayshott CE Primary School, Grayshott

All About Me

J am is my favourite
A pples are my favourite fruit
M y favourite colour is red
I love playing football
E xcellent at maths.

Jamie Pinchbeck (7)
Hareleeshill Primary School, Larkhall

I Am Layla

L ovely, loyal Layla is my name
A lways ready to help read
Y o-yos are my favourite toy
L ovely Lucy is my friend
A lways here to help.

Layla Colby (7)
Hermitage Primary School, Hermitage

Ana Laura - This Is Me

A mazing
N ice
A thlete

L ovely
A wesome
U nderstanding
R ocking
A ngelic.

Ana Laura Hawkins (6)
Hermitage Primary School, Hermitage

Georgia

G ive good hugs
E lephants are my favourite
O ranges are delicious
R eally love giving hugs
G eorgia is always happy
I love my nana, she makes me happy
A lways tidies up.

Georgia Clarke (6)
Latchford St James CE Primary School, Warrington

Mia

M y best friend is Mam
I like to play with my brother, Oscar
A lways playing Minecraft.

Mia Ko (7)
Latchford St James CE Primary School, Warrington

Isabella

I s kind and helpful
S hares all things
A nnoys Ruby
B right and cheerful
E ats lovely sweets
L ikes to play
L oves Mummy
A sks lots of questions.

Isabella Gabbey (6)
Londonderry Primary School, Newtownards

Max

T ries hard
E ats lovely food
D o things
D o things
Y awns when tired.

Max Johnson (6)
Londonderry Primary School, Newtownards

Niko

N ever complains
I s kind and helpful
K eeps work neat
O wns lots of toys.

Niko Newell (6)
Londonderry Primary School, Newtownards

Maisie

M y name is Maisie and I am very happy
A nother day I was as happy as can be
I am very kind
S ometimes I can be mean
I am friendly
E lephants are my fifth favourite animal.

Maisie Bryce (7)
Low Port Primary School, Linlithgow

Blaine

B laine is my name, I like it
L ions in South Africa are cool
A wesome is what I am
I like visiting my grandparents
N uts are nice
E arth is cool.

Blaine Brodie (7)
Low Port Primary School, Linlithgow

Maili

M aili is my name and I am very happy
A dog is my pet
I like my best friends, Eva and Julia
L ove is beautiful
I am respectful.

Maili MacKenzie (7)
Low Port Primary School, Linlithgow

Isla

I sla is my name and my friend is Iona
S ome people in my class are kind
L ove is special
A day I liked was when I went to the zoo.

Isla Park (6)
Low Port Primary School, Linlithgow

Eva

E va is my name, I was born at Easter
V iolet is my fourth favourite colour
A zebra is my favourite animal.

Eva Ogg (7)
Low Port Primary School, Linlithgow

Max

M y name is Max and I am excited
A koala is my favourite animal
e **X** cited is my feeling.

Max Meecham (7)
Low Port Primary School, Linlithgow

Zac

Z ac is my name
A sheep is furry
C heep cheep a chicken goes.

Zac Buchanan (7)
Low Port Primary School, Linlithgow

Lillianna

L ove my mummy.
I am beautiful.
L ike my friends.
L earn at school.
I am good at waiting in line
A nd I am polite.
N ever went to swimming.
N ever went to dancing
A nd I like my daddy.

Lillianna Holmes (7)
Millbank Primary School, Buckie

Maddison

M agnificent at maths
A fraid of spiders
D etermined
D aring
I nventive and creative
S kips with a rope
O ranges are my favourite
N ever stop talking.

Maddison Smith (7)
Millbank Primary School, Buckie

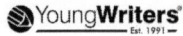

Logan

L ikes to play games
O utside
G ood fun
A lways tries his best
N ever has a phone.

Logan Mitchell (6)
Millbank Primary School, Buckie

Bria

B rilliant at singing.
R eady for bed.
I nterested in dogs.
A nimals are great.

Bria Hildreth (7)
Millbank Primary School, Buckie

Brave, Love, Eat

B right
R esilient
A dventures
V entures
E xcellent

L ikeable
O ctopus
V ision
E at

E xcellent
A ble to climb
T errific.

Julian Bueno Sanchez (6)
Moldgreen Community Primary, Moldgreen

Sporty, Brave

S ensible
P layful
O utgoing
R esilient
T idy
Y oung

B right
R esilient
A mazing
V ery nice
E xcellent.

Maksymilian Pisarczyk (6)
Moldgreen Community Primary, Moldgreen

Happy Me

H elpful and fun
A ctive and healthy
P repared to learn
P retty ponytails
Y oung and clever.

Sophie Elliott (6)
Moldgreen Community Primary, Moldgreen

Happy Me

H elpful
A girl and fit
P roud
P erfect pupil
Y oung and ready to learn.

Dayan Ravesh (6)
Moldgreen Community Primary, Moldgreen

Happy Me

H elpful pupil
A n active boy
P layful boy
P laying boy
Y ummy food.

Miracle Ayeni (6)
Moldgreen Community Primary, Moldgreen

Brave

B rave
R esponsible
A wake
V ery
E xcited.

Inayah Akhtar (7)
Moldgreen Community Primary, Moldgreen

Love

L ovely
O range
V ery kind
E xcellent.

Kenzie Atkinson (6)
Moldgreen Community Primary, Moldgreen

Kind

K itten
I nteresting
N ights
D awns.

Lily Rose Mitchell (6)
Moldgreen Community Primary, Moldgreen

Nice

N ice
I ce cream
C alm
E nergetic.

Cole Dyer (6)
Moldgreen Community Primary, Moldgreen

Nice

N ame
I ce cream
C old
E lephant.

Mahnoor Fatima (6)
Moldgreen Community Primary, Moldgreen

Summer

S wimming in my paddling pool.
U pon a plane to go away.
M ummy buys me an ice cream.
M emories made at the beach.
E xtremely hot and warm.
R iding my bike by the seaside.

Açelya Ecem Aziz (7)
North Crescent Primary School, Wickford

Winter

W inter is freezing cold.
I cicles hang up high.
N ew gloves and jackets are worn.
T rees are bare of leaves.
E verything is freezing.
R oasting fire to stay warm.

Zachary DeLeon (6)
North Crescent Primary School, Wickford

Pizza

P izza has lots of cheese
I like pizza when it's hot
Z ooming good pizza
Z igzag crust
A pizza has tomatoes under the cheese.

Jake Crowe (6)
Oak View Primary & Nursery School, Hatfield

Football

F ootball is the best
O n Sunday, I go to football
O verjoyed when they win
T eagen is my teammate
B all tricks are easy
A fter September
L ove to watch Man Utd play
L ove to play a match.

Archie Sarvar (6)
Park Lane Primary School, Tilehurst

Darcie

D arcie is a good friend
A lways nice
R eally kind
C aring person
I s really helpful
E veryone likes Darcie.

Darcie Hook (6)
Park Lane Primary School, Tilehurst

Happy Me

H aving fun with friends
A mazing at swimming
P laying football
P ositive attitude
Y ay! I'm so happy!

Edwin Libin (5)
Parkhill Primary School, Leven

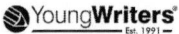

Puppy Love

P erfect little bundles
U nder their mother's body
P aws are so small
P ink little tongues
I nside the house is their playground
E ars are so sharp, they can hear every sound
S o much love and laughter when you have puppies.

Amelia Butt (5)
Parkinson Lane Community Primary School, Halifax

Things That Make Me Smile

S chool is fun
M ornings in the sun
I n the playground, playing tig
L earning new things
E njoyable times that make me smile.

Aminah Ali (6)
Parkinson Lane Community Primary School, Halifax

Dance

D ancing is my hobby
A nice sunny day
N o one hates parties
C ould you dance with me, please?
E njoy your hobby.

Sana Elcarazeh (7)
Parkinson Lane Community Primary School, Halifax

Mummy

M ummy is kind
U mbrellas are good in the rain
M oon is in the sky
M onkey on the tree
Y ou are the best teacher.

Shan Abdulla (6)
Parkinson Lane Community Primary School, Halifax

Fresh Fruit

F resh fruit
R ed strawberry
U nhappy grapes
I nteresting fruits
T ough banana.

Armaan Moghul (5)
Parkinson Lane Community Primary School, Halifax

Inayah

I ntelligent
N ice
A mazing
Y oung
A smart girl
H appy.

Inayah Hussain (5)
Parkinson Lane Community Primary School, Halifax

Friend

F unny
R ocky
I ntelligent
E xciting
N oisy
D iva.

Hoorain Hassan (5)
Parkinson Lane Community Primary School, Halifax

Cats Are The Best

K ind cats are my favourite animal
I magination is big
N ever say never
D o kind things and have a kind heart.

Lilliana Money (6)
Robsack Wood Primary Academy, St Leonards-On-Sea

Cats

C ats are cute
A nd they like food
T hey sleep all day
S o let's go out.

Alfie Goldsmith (6)
Robsack Wood Primary Academy, St Leonards-On-Sea

All About Me

H ave two sisters
A lot of chocolate for me
W atermelon is my favourite fruit
W ith my sisters, I like to shop
A mazing at singing.

Hawwa Alshareef (7)
Seaton School, Aberdeen

Things I Like

D inosaurs are the best
A nimals are my favourite
V ery good at basketball
I love ice cream
D oing Xbox all day long.

David Emmanuel (7)
Seaton School, Aberdeen

About Tima

T oo fast
I love music
M y favourite colour is red
A lways playing.

Tymofii Karpenko (7)
Seaton School, Aberdeen

About Leo

L ove Minecraft
E njoys McDonald's
O range juice is my favourite.

Leo Wilson (6)
Seaton School, Aberdeen

Football

F un is football
O utside is where it is
O verhead kicks are my fave
T aking penalties I love to do
B ackward kicks I can do
A nd I can throw very far
L ong runs are what we do
L oving football.

Ayyan Malik (6)
St George's Primary School, Glasgow

This Is Me

E very time my mum rocks me
L ove my granda
L ets me play with paint
A nd make lots of pictures

M e and Granda have dinner
A lso we play together
E ven play football.

Ella Mae McNicol (6)
St George's Primary School, Glasgow

Concerts

C oncerts are my fave
O utside they are
N oisy music is the best
C oming with my family
E very day tickets are on
R eal live concerts
T ickets booked.

Eva Minalescu (7)
St George's Primary School, Glasgow

Xbox

X box is the thing to do always
B lasts out noise from my room
O n it are really good games
X box is my favourite thing.

Harry Carey (7)
St George's Primary School, Glasgow

Dogs

D ogs are the best pet
O utside is where we walk them
G oing on a leash for a walk
S o we think dogs are better.

Ethan (6)
St George's Primary School, Glasgow

Rainbow

R ainbows make me happy
A nd always make me smile
I love to spot a rainbow
N ever-ending rainbows
B rightly shining through the clouds
O ver the hills and stretching far
W hat a pretty sight you are.

Leona Baos (7)
St Joseph's Primary School, Gabalfa

Poem

P oems are the best
O ur friends are the best friends in the world
E veryone is my friend
M y favourite is football!

Divine Esuku (7)
St Joseph's Primary School, Gabalfa

Mommy

M oms are loving
O verprotective
M ine is my hero
M aking the best meals
Y ummy food always.

Zoe Ekere (6)
St Joseph's Primary School, Gabalfa

Evie

E vie likes toys
V alentine's is the best day
I nsects are the best
E vie likes babies.

Evie Fox (6)
St Michael With St Thomas Primary School, Widnes

Lexi

L icking ice cream
E vie is my friend
e **X** ploring is amazing
I ce cream.

Lexi Davies (7)
St Michael With St Thomas Primary School, Widnes

Michaela

M aking cakes and buns
I love my teddy, Dede
C an I go to Donegal?
H olidays by the beach
A rts and crafts
E va is my friend
L oves sweets and treats
A t home with my family.

Michaela McGirr (6)
St Patrick's Primary School, Eskra

Cadhan

C ows and tractors
A nd diggers too
D riving them around the farm
H elping Granda
A nd Daddy too
N othing more I love to do.

Cadhan Gallagher (6)
St Patrick's Primary School, Eskra

Happy Gold Egg

H eart
A pple
P rince
P lay
Y ou are the best

G eorgie
O livia
L aney
D elicious

E gg
G oing to get
G o to the shop.

Olivia Fox (6)
St Philip's CE Primary School, Atherton

Avaya

A vaya is my bestest friend
V ery good TikTok dances
A good friend
Y ou are a good gymnast
A chocolate lover.

Isaac Calderbank (7)
St Philip's CE Primary School, Atherton

My Favourite Hobby

R acing is my favourite sport
U nder my bed is my best toy
N ehemiah is my friend
N ani is my favourite player
I love my friends
N apping is healthy for us
G ymnastics is my favourite.

Ali Saddique (7)
St Stephen's CE Primary School, West Bowling

Football

F ast I am
O utdoors
O ver the bar
T eams
B all
A im
L augh
L ong shot.

Mohammad Hanzalah (6)
St Stephen's CE Primary School, West Bowling

This Is Me

E hab loves glasses
H ome is my favourite place
A pples are a healthy food
B all sports are my favourite sports.

Ehab Sanattin (6)
St Stephen's CE Primary School, West Bowling

Haris

H appy boy
A nd very clever
R onaldo is my idol
I am going to be like him
S uperstar footballer.

Haris Akhtar (6)
St Stephen's CE Primary School, West Bowling

Sara

S cared of spiders
A nnoying sister
R unning is my favourite
A lways ready to learn new things.

Sara Al-Hourani (7)
St Stephen's CE Primary School, West Bowling

Happy

H ugs make me happy because I feel cared for
A rran playing with me makes me happy
P laying makes me happy because it makes me laugh
P ractising my football at the astros makes me happy
Y ellow is a happy colour and it's a sign of happiness.

Corry Gray (7)
Struthers Primary School, Muirhead

Happy

H appiness comes from happy hearts
A rt is a happy time to relax and share
P laying a polite game is a sign of happiness
P hoebe is a polite person and she is happiness
Y ellow is the happy side, yellow is the brightest.

Lewis Ritchie
Struthers Primary School, Muirhead

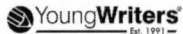

All About Lochlan

L ove my family
O h, I am strong
C alvin is my favourite brother
H appiness is my favourite feeling
L ove my friends
A pple juice is my favourite drink
N ever stop smiling.

Lochlan Keenan (7)
Struthers Primary School, Muirhead

Happy

H ugs from my family make me happy
A rt and colouring make me happy
P ies are tasty and make me happy
P iling up winter leaves makes me happy
Y ummy bananas make me happy.

Callum Wilson (8)
Struthers Primary School, Muirhead

Happy

H appiness is full of love
A rt makes me happy because it is fun
P ippa is my best friend forever
P uppies make me happy because they are soft
Y ou make me happy!

Phoebe Coxon (7)
Struthers Primary School, Muirhead

Happy

H ugs from my family make me feel cared for
A rran plays with me and it makes me happy
P laying makes me laugh
P izza makes me smile
Y ellow is a happy colour.

Max Wilson (8)
Struthers Primary School, Muirhead

Happy

H olidays make me happy
A ll of my friends are kind
P laying is fun
P arks make me smile
Y ummy apple pie.

Zara Townsend
Struthers Primary School, Muirhead

Laila

L ovely
A pples
I ce lollies
L oves double-decker buses
A lways playing.

Laila Jasim (5)
The John Wallis CE Academy, Kingsnorth

Dane

D aring
A policeman
N ice
E nergetic.

Dane Court (5)
The John Wallis CE Academy, Kingsnorth

Adam

A good gamer
D uck
A wesome
M ummy.

Adam Miah (5)
The John Wallis CE Academy, Kingsnorth

Halloween

H aribos with chocolate are my favourite
A ll dressed up in costumes
L aughing all along
L ooking for sweets
O ut in the moonlight
W itches are showing off
E vil queen dressed up
E ating pumpkin soup
N ever forget Halloween.

Amerleigh Feeley (7)
Windale Primary School, Greater Leys

Football

F ootball
O n the pitch
O ff the pitch
T ackling
B all flies through the sky
A ll players score a goal
L ots of people
L ots of goals.

Cordell Massey-Matthews (6)
Windale Primary School, Greater Leys

Summer

S wimming in the water
U p and down in the water
M y turn to jump into the water
M e too
E verybody, let's all jump at the same time!
R io can join us!

Leonardo Hyseni-Curtis (6)
Windale Primary School, Greater Leys

Sonic

S uper speed
O ut of this world
N o Eggman
I n Green Hill Zone
C atch Metal Sonic.

Ali Nasir (6)
Windale Primary School, Greater Leys

Young Writers Information

We hope you have enjoyed reading this book – and that you will continue to in the coming years.

If you're the parent or family member of an enthusiastic poet or story writer, do visit **www.youngwriters.co.uk/subscribe** and sign up to receive news, competitions, writing challenges and tips, activities and much, much more! There's lots to keep budding writers motivated!

If you would like to order further copies of this book, or any of our other titles, then please give us a call or order via your online account.

Young Writers
Remus House
Coltsfoot Drive
Peterborough
PE2 9BF
(01733) 890066
info@youngwriters.co.uk

Join in the conversation!
Tips, news, giveaways and much more!

 YoungWritersUK   YoungWritersCW   youngwriterscw

Scan me to watch the This Is Me video!